7.50

A MATERIALIST'S
RELIGION

A MATERIALIST'S RELIGION

by Shigeru Abe

MIYABI SHOBO
Tokyo

The letter "I" in the center of the logo for Miyabi Shobo represents the self; the vortex swirling around it stands for the Milky Way, which surrounds the earth. Together they symbolize the universe. The mark as a whole is a symbolic representation of mankind's cosmic life, through which he lives by being given life.

Translation by Jeffrey Hunter. Production supervision by John Weatherhill, Inc., New York and Tokyo.

First edition, 1986

Published by Miyabi Shobo, 1-7-14 Takadanobaba, Shinjuku-ku, Tokyo 160. Copyright © by Shigeru Abe. All rights reserved. Printed in Japan.   ISBN 4-943838-01-4

The Mind of One Finger

My search for the True Life—the life that lives of itself—began when I experienced the truth that I am given life.

The cosmos itself lives of itself.

If I liken the cosmos to a human body, my own self is no more than a single finger on that great cosmic body.

Let us assume that single finger has a mind. Our minds are no more than that.

Contents

Foreword

"The True Religion That Transcends Life and Death"

The author of this book bravely confronted the seemingly inevitable approach of death and, by calmly preparing himself and deep introspection, achieved the hard-won state of joy in the Dharma, to which he has given form in this short work. This is not simply another book, but the unstoppable cry of a living soul. It is the compassionate act of one who wishes to spread the truth of "the cosmic life of human beings, living and given life." In it is grasped the eternal life that may seem to be extinguished but never is, may seem to be born but is not. I recommend it as an experiential religious account that, with its convincing use of the knowledge of modern science, the people of our age will find persuasive. After reading it they will awaken to the fact that they are given life by the eternal life that transcends the dichotomy of life and death, and the peace of mind this awakening provides will bring a new life to their daily activities.

Is the author really the materialist he claims to be? I

encounter here a True Man of No Rank passing through the world of the identity of matter and mind, a self-enlightened, independent, Practitioner of the Way.

Sobin Yamada
Head Priest of the Shinju-an
Daitokuji, Kyoto

Preface

The road by which the materialist approaches religion leads through a very narrow gate. This book is a record of the difficulties of my attempt, as a materialist, to grasp and formulate a religion I could believe in. For what can religion mean to the materialist? Before investigating that problem, however, I must describe the process through which this book came to be. I wrote the table of contents and chapters 1 through 3 more than thirty years ago, when I was in my thirties. Since it was composed as a journal of my thoughts at the time, I have not modified it in any fashion, but present what I wrote then exactly as it is. The remaining chapters were composed from May to October 1978, following the table of contents of thirty years before. It was my goal, at age sixty-four, to complete this treatise faithful to my intentions of three decades ago.

The Afterword contains my own, present reflections on what I wrote, based on my studies of Buddhism over the years. Since 1951 I have been busily occupied with a career as a certified public accountant. For many years I had little opportunity to read books on religion. When, recently, I began my studies again, I found that Japanese research on early Buddhism has progressed remarkably since World War II. Early Buddhism is the Buddhism that was taught directly by the historical personage Shakyamuni and recorded in scriptures after his death by his disciples. The Buddhism that we in Japan are most familiar with is Mahayana Buddhism, which developed at a later period from early Buddhism. My discovery of this whole new world of Buddhist thought has been a great comfort and inspiration to me, and its influences are to be seen in my Afterword, so I think it appropriate to broadly trace its outlines here.

Dr. Fumio Masutani, a scholar of early Buddhism whose work has been of considerable inspiration to me, organizes the differences between early Buddhism and Mahayana Buddhism under these five issues: (1) the individual versus the masses; (2) analysis versus direct insight; (3) the arhat ideal versus the bodhisattva ideal; (4) consciousness versus unconsciousness; and (5) logical principles versus emotions. For our purposes, it is not necessary to explore these distinctions individually. What is unique is Dr. Masutani's conclusion: that the tensions between early Buddhism and Mahayana Buddhism can and should be resolved from a new perspective, an existential perspective. He holds that any of these tensions will be resolved if they are reflected upon deeply from the existential point of view—the actual perspective of the experience of human beings living in the world.

After studies of works such as those of Dr. Masutani, I looked back over what I had written, and noticed my own mixture of analysis and direct intuition. Of course, my analysis was not the minute and detailed analysis of early Buddhism, nor were my intuitions the profound and penetrating ones of Mahayana. The second and third chapters consisted, it seemed to me, mostly of analysis, while chapter 4 contained a record of my direct intuition. Yet it was the intuition that came to me first, and the analysis was born from that. The two together grew to form this book, *A Materialist's Religion*, in its final shape.

In its simplest form, my direct intuition was that we

do not live, but are kept alive. The feeling of living was merely an illusion of the mind, while the fact was that I was given life—when I realized this an untold joy and gratitude gripped my heart and filled my whole being.

After that I turned myself to the task of analyzing the way in which the human body was kept alive. By this means I became aware of the true scope of human life, and awakened to the identity of self and others. Another analysis I attempted was to discover the way in which the human mind was formed. By this means I was able to learn the source of the illusion that the self is living its own life, when in fact it is being kept alive by others.

After attaining this direct intuition and embarking on this analysis, I found myself reading books on religion with a new, open attitude that I did not possess before.

More than thirty years have passed since this process began. Now that this book is completed, I realize that it was my Buddhist primer. I look forward to continued study and to seeing how in my own life I am able to reconcile the differences between early and Mahayana Buddhism as pointed out by Dr. Masutani. Before closing this Preface, I would like to present Dr. Masutani's discussion of two verses on the dharma of dependent co-arising (Japanese, *engi;* Sanskrit, *pratityasamutpada*) which was the starting point of the Buddha's enlightenment, because I think it justifies and clarifies my "materialist" viewpoint from a Buddhist stance, and shows how close it is to basic Buddhist assumptions.

One sutra speaks of the Buddha's enlightenment experience in the following verse: "When the saint contemplated with great concentration / All the manifold dharmas became clear / And all his doubts disappeared / Because he realized the principle of dependent co-arising." The term dependent co-arising is an interesting one. . . . It means, clearly, that all arises depending upon conditions. The principle indicated by this term is the law realized by Gautama Buddha that governs the manifold dharmas (all existence). He grasped the fact, after sitting in concentrated contemplation under the Bodhi tree, that all existence is permeated by the principle of dependent co-arising.

The second verse is as follows:

> According to another scripture, the Buddha remained in concentration under the Bodhi tree for some time after attaining full enlightenment. The first thing he did at this time was to organize the principle of dependent co-arising in the following verse formula: "Depending upon that, this exists / Depending on the birth of that, this is born / Depending on the absence of that, this is absent / Depending on the disappearance of that, this disappears." I call this the formula of dependent co-arising, because the Buddha afterward always applied this formula to considerations on the subject of the self. The subject that the Buddha was preoccupied with when he left his home to become a seeker was the problem of birth, old age, sickness, and death—or, in abbreviated form, old age and death. In even more distilled form, the subject was suffering. It was this subject to which he first applied the formula of dependent co-arising.

Here Dr. Masutani is describing the very entrance to the path that leads to enlightenment, I believe. I would like to quote a bit more from his writings, one anecdote each that illustrates the two aspects of Buddhist philosophy, the theories of cause and effect and of existence. The first is as follows:

The *Avatamsaka Sutra* explains this principle through the metaphor of Indra's net. Indra . . . was one of the highest gods of the ancient Hindu pantheon. . . . Indra was thought to possess a great net that covered our entire world. It was woven of an infinite number of warp and woof threads, and a jewel was hung at each of their interstices. When one jewel was shaken, all the rest moved. The scripture uses this metaphor to describe the infinite overlapping of relationships in our universe. This is the Buddhist view of the world we live in.

The second passage is from the *Samyutta Nikaya,* a scripture that has left a great impression on me:

He was, as always, in retreat at Jetagaya, when he said: "O monks! I will teach you about the all." And he called them together and said the following. "O monks, what is the all? It is the eye and form, the ear and sound, the nose and scent, the tongue and taste, the body and texture, the mind and dharma. O monks, this we call the all. O monks! Should there be a person who says that he will tell you of another all beyond this all, those are only empty words, and he will be unable to reply to the criticisms of others, and he will eventually fall into difficulties. Why is that? O monks, it is because his all is not a thing of this world." The sutra quoted above is a short one that has been largely overlooked up till now, but I would like to call attention to it. The theory of perception presented here seems at first very naive, yet it shows clearly that Gautama Buddha was a thinker who considered the structure of the human consciousness and pondered the relationship between man and existence.

Sources

The following books have been of great help to me in the composition of this work. I have quoted and paraphrased from them, but more than that they have been my spiritual leaders along the path I continue to walk. I wish to express my gratitude to their authors, both living and dead, for their guidance.

Japanese Revised New Testament. Tokyo: American Bible Society.

Rissho Kosei Kai Fukyo Honbu, ed. *Hokekyo no Meiku.* Tokyo: Kosei Shuppansha, 1973.

Rissho Kosei Kai Kyogakubu, ed. *Bukkyo no Hongi.* Tokyo: Kosei Shuppansha, 1966.

Shaku Soen. *Saikontan Kowa.* Tokyo: Bunichi Shuppan, 1975.

Shoyo Tsubouchi, trans. *Hamlet, Prince of Denmark.*

Tazato Yakumu. *Dogen Zen Nyumon.* Tokyo: Sangyo Noritsu Daigaku Shuppanbu, 1978.

A MATERIALIST'S
RELIGION

1
Religion for the Materialist

The Kingdom of Heaven is like to a grain of mustard seed, which man took, and sowed in his field:
Which is indeed the least of all seeds: but when it is grown, it is the greatest among herbs, and becometh a tree, so that the birds of the air come and lodge in the branches thereof.

Matthew 13:31–32

The Kingdom of Heaven is like unto leaven, which a woman took, and hid in three measures of meal, till the whole was leavened.

Matthew 13:33

These words of the New Testament leave no doubt as to the great benefits of faith in the Kingdom of Heaven. Unfortunately, though the blessings of the Kingdom of Heaven are great, they can have no effect at all unless the faith is firmly planted in the minds of men. And to believe in the Kingdom of Heaven is not any easy thing. It is not something that can be accomplished by everyone.

Many years ago when I was battling with tuberculosis, I acquired several religious books to try to ease the mental anguish I was suffering. But all of them preached the supremacy of the mind over matter. One of them said that all matter was a mere reflection of the mind, and that the body and its illnesses existed if we thought they did, and did not if we did not. Yet however great my sufferings, I could not accept this insistence on the total supremacy of the mind. It was impossible for me, aware even to the small degree that I was of modern scientific thought, to believe in the existence of a Christian heaven or a Buddhist Pure Land in the west where my mind would go and live after my death.

Since faith is the absolute necessity in religion, those of us who are unable to have faith are shut out from the great blessings of the Kingdom of Heaven. Still, life's sufferings visit us with unflagging persistence. We face the difficulties of illness, of earning a living, of getting along with each other, and finally, of dying. Whether we believe in God or not, whether we have great aspirations or lack them, at some time or other life suddenly pushes us in a totally unanticipated and not always desirable direction. Anyone who finds himself suddenly in painful circumstances suffers. Perhaps those who believe in God are saved from such sufferings sooner than most, due to the great blessings of the Kingdom of Heaven. Some of the faithless as well will no doubt wish to reap the benefits of the Kingdom of God, and endeavor to have faith in God and his heaven. But it is very difficult to find faith by such a conscious act of will. One doesn't acquire faith through the decision to believe. No matter with what determination we decide "I will believe in this god," unless faith truly wells up from the deepest source of the heart, the blessings of the Kingdom of God are not bestowed on us. So it is that those who for one reason or another do not have faith can never feel the ecstasy of religious joy nor be saved from the trials that trouble the human heart.

I write this book for those in search of religion who cannot find it and for those who strive for faith yet find themselves unable to believe. Herein I present a religion that is established not by faith but by understanding, not by belief in God but by knowledge of him.

2
Understanding God

Since the religion I propose is not one of faith but of understanding, instead of enjoining man to have faith in God I urge understanding of the divine. How can we understand God? Let me begin by outlining here the method I propose to understand the divine.

First we must understand clearly the manner in which the processes of human life work. Next we must clarify the nature of the human mind and spirit. After we know the natures of human life and the human mind, we must consider the relationship between them. At that point we will discover a great contradiction, a contradiction that arises from the gap between the scope of human life and the scope of the mind, and a contradiction that no human being can escape. This contradiction, we will learn, is the very source of all human sufferings, the cause of the unending conflicts that plague human existence. What we must understand, in other words, is that there exists a gap between the realms of our lives and our minds that presents us with an existential dilemma. Once we have come to grips with this, a self that we have been completely unaware of up to now will become apparent to us. And with knowledge of ourselves comes knowledge of God. Now let us move on to the details of these matters. We must begin by observing the human life process itself.

A well-known passage in *Hamlet* offers us an apt description of human life. The following lines from act IV, scene 3, are spoken after Hamlet has stabbed Polonius, who was spying on him.

King: Now Hamlet, where's Polonius?
Hamlet: At supper.
King: At supper! Where?
Hamlet: Not where he eats, but where he is eaten: a certain convocation of politic worms are e'en at him. Your worm is your only emperor for diet: we fat all creatures else to fat us, and we fat ourselves for maggots: your fat king and your lean beggar is but variable service, two dishes, but to one table: that's the end.
King: Alas, alas!
Hamlet: A man may fish with the worm that eat of a king, and eat of the fish that hath fed of that worm.
King: What dost thou mean by this?
Hamlet: Nothing but to show you how a king may go a progress through the guts of a beggar.

Only a madman such as Hamlet could utter such seeming nonsense; and yet, at the risk of being taken for a madman myself, I would like to consider the phenomena of our world from this standpoint for a while.

Hamlet vividly describes the progress of the man whose corpse is eaten by worms that then serve as bait for fish, which in turn is eaten by a beggar. I wish to extend that argument to its logical conclusion and emphasize that the same thing is happening to our own living bodies as well, minute by minute, hour by hour. Through what sort of processes is this occurring?

Each time I exhale, some of my cells leave the body as carbon dioxide. The carbon dioxide is then absorbed by the leaves of a plant and becomes a part of that plant's body. When that plant is eaten by a cow, the cell that was once part of my body contributes to the growth of the cow. The cow is killed for human consumption and is eaten by a king—or a beggar, for that matter. The cell may then leave the human body as excrement and go on to fertilize a radish, a carrot, or some other vegetable. Or, if the man dies, it may go on to feed worms, as Hamlet has it. In that case it might be cast in the ocean and become part of a fish, which might in turn become a part of a human body again.

What composes my body today might be air tomorrow, drifting on its way across the ocean to America. There it might become a vegetable, be packed in a can, transported across the American continent, and finally make its way into the body of a Frenchman or a German. The matter which makes up the human body moves from one body to another, as well as from a human body to a plant, and from a plant to an animal body. The cells of our body may burrow underground, float away on the waters, rise up into the clouds, or burn in a crackling flame. There is no way to prevent their ceaseless motion.

This is the simplest of descriptions. With a little imaginative speculation, many other possibilities present themselves. At any rate, the matter which makes up this five-foot-several-inch body of some 125 pounds is not by any means my exclusive possession. If I try to make it so, I will only perish. Likewise, the matter that makes up your body is not your exclusive possession. Some portion of the matter which makes up our bodies is continually leaving our bodies, and other matter from outside is continually replenishing our bodies. This phenomenon we call metabolism. Metabolism, however, refers only to the processes that occur within an organism. I have traced the substances that are leaving my body moment by moment and followed them to their destinations. And thus I have learned that they are our common possession.

They are, in fact, the common possession of all mankind, all animals, all living things. I am not saying that my body becomes the possession of another being after my death. What I am saying is that even while I am alive my body belongs to other beings. And, in turn, the body you now occupy is also my common possession. This is the nature of our life process, reflection on which is the starting point of all religions.

Next let us consider, from a somewhat wider viewpoint, existence beyond the earth. Without the sun, the earth we live on could not exist. The solar system itself exists in its present form supported by a balance of the forces of infinite numbers of other stars. When we consider such phenomena as cosmic rays, it becomes clear that the ways in which our lives might be influenced by existences far beyond our own solar system are difficult to even imagine.

What does all this teach us? It can only mean this: my life process is taking place on a universal scale. Yours is too. The life processes of all humans living on the earth are taking place on a cosmic scale. And not only human lives, but the life processes of all living things, animals and plants, unfold on a cosmic scale. Nor can inanimate matter, which is what gives life to living things, be excluded from the phenomena of life. If a human life is severed from the outside world that is its setting, it expires at once. If we try to limit our scope to this five-foot-several-inch body, we find that it has no existence in time, but remains a simple, three-dimensional space. A self that exists only in three dimensions, like a photographic image, is dead. When we move into a four-dimensional world, in which time is added to the previous three dimensions, and regard our self, we find ourselves forced to expand the scope of our life to the universal scale elaborated earlier.

There can be only one life process on the cosmic scale we are imagining. All the infinite "individual" lives are identical to it or revert to it. This is the import of religious mysticism, and here I might be accused of approaching mysticism myself. Nor do the words "All the infinite lives revert to the one" find a responsive chord in everyone's heart, I am sure. Though the reasoning might be convincing, our hearts don't agree, and we find the logic suspect, as if we have been cleverly deceived. Why is this? It will become clear once we have understood the manner in which the human mind is formed, a subject that I will discuss in the next chapter.

3

The Human Mind

In the previous chapter I explained how the life processes of us humans and all living things are carried out on a cosmic scale. Anyone who studies and observes the phenomena of the universe in an unemotional, scientific manner will come to this conclusion. Yet when we think of life we tend to identify it with the separate lives that appear to be somehow "within" the bodies of individual organisms. For most people, life processes go on only inside the bodies of living things. They never dare to conceive of a life process that takes place outside the body.

Of course the subject matter of the life sciences is just these life processes that take place within organisms, and there is nothing wrong with considering the phenomena of life from that viewpoint. But since our goal is to understand what religion is, we must add certain reflections to this biological view of life, reflections that for our common sense are extremely difficult to grasp. They are the root of the difficulty with which religion always presents us. The cause of the difficulty in reflecting on our view of life lies in the very origins of the mind. It is for that reason that I have speculated on the development of the human mind in the following pages.

The human mind consists of the activity of the brain. A scientific explanation of the exact relationship between the brain and the mind would be very difficult. I am neither a scientist nor a doctor, and lack the ability to explain it. I must leave that task to the specialist. Here we can only discuss it in the simplest, common-sense terms.

When we search for the reasons for the development of our brains, the first that presents itself is that the sensory impressions received by our nerves throughout the body are all channeled to the brain. At first the brain does not have the power to interpret those impressions, but merely records and stores them. After a rich store of sense impressions has accumulated, the brain becomes able, little by little, to determine the meaning of the impressions it receives from the body's nerve centers. The stored information grows and grows as impressions accumulate and are synthesized and interpreted, and those very interpretations are stored as new data as well. In this process of receiving, interpreting, and storing information, the activity of our brain develops to a high level.

Our minds are nothing but these highly developed brain functions. Human brain functions are far more advanced than those of any other animal. With our minds we can consider being and nonbeing, love and hate, profit and loss, good and evil, and all the phenomena of the external world. Our minds have even developed to the point where they can consider themselves. Yet however highly developed the human mind is, it remains a function of the brain's activity, and the brain is a development based on the sensations received by the nerves of the physical body. Our minds, in other words, are built on the foundations of our bodies.

Because our minds are a development from our physical bodies, it is extremely natural that our minds should regard our physical bodies as our selves. The mind regards the body as the self, the body's life as its life, and experiences everything from within the framework of the flesh. This is all the natural result of the fact that the mind is a product of the body. As far as our mind is concerned, the scope of our life is no greater than the scope of our physical body. It conceives of our life as coequal to that of the body, flourishing as the body flourishes and failing as the body fails. We believe this from the time we are born, and, indeed, most people believe this until the very end. As a rule man never awakens to the fact of the grand scale of the life process, as described in the previous chapter; instead he dreams away his brief existence in an ignorant stupor.

Those who would think about religion or consider the problems of existence must transcend all concepts plagued by the pitfalls described above. The commonly held belief that this meagre body is our true body, that the life of the physical body is our true life, is nothing but an illusion, one of the pitfalls of the senses, when the true life process is known. The reason that so few people recognize the illusion for what it is, is that our mind is based on the very illusory senses that create the illusion.

I wish to point out that it is an illusion to identify the physical life as my true life, and offer this one question in order to encourage others to reflect on the proper way of looking at human life: Does this body live its life, or is it actually kept alive? Of course the average person will answer, "The life of the body is a living thing." But if we understand the life process in its totality, as described in the previous chapter, it is clear that we cannot say so easily that the body is living. When limiting ourselves to the scale of the physical body, it is certainly more appropriate to say that it is kept alive. What is this "living" that we so lightly speak of? Careful observation of the actual processes shows that we have simply called "being kept alive" living. The hasty conclusion that this physical life that is being kept alive is actually living of its own accord is an illusion of our minds. The reason for the illusion is that our minds are based on and develop from the sense perceptions of the physical body.

Let us think of the universe as a single human body. This person has a very strange anatomy, in that all sensation is concentrated in one tiny portion of the body, the rest of which is insensate. Let's say that the concentration of nerve endings is found in the index finger of the left hand. Because of the presence of nerves and sense perceptions, this left-hand index finger develops a mind of its own. It is only natural that this newly born mind will think that the left-hand index finger, and it alone, is its body. The mind of the index finger will not realize that it is being kept alive by the entire body, and will no doubt entertain the illusion that it lives its own independent life. Although of course what is really living is the entire body, and the index finger is only kept alive as a part of the whole, it firmly believes it lives on its own and does not recognize the greater life given to it by and shared by the entire body.

As discussed earlier, our true life as human beings is carried out on a cosmic scale; I have likened the "body" that is living this greater life to a single human being. Within this metaphor, the human body is likened to a single finger of the great cosmic body. Just as a single finger is alive because the blood of the entire body courses through it, our bodies are kept alive through the constant passage of air and water and foodstuffs through them. Our minds, which are the products of the nerves of our bodies, are, to the great cosmic body, like the mind of the single finger, based solely on the sensations available to that single finger. It is extremely difficult for this meagre "one-finger" mind of ours to see our true, entire body.

In other words, what we regard as our existence is actually an existence that is given to us. We do not live, but are kept alive. Our mind, the product of our body, sees only the given existence. It cannot see the giving existence. With this handicap, it concludes that what is being kept alive is living of its own. Yet this is, as I have said again and again, an illusion based on the nature of perception. All living things on the earth are given life by the same great life. Still we neglect to think of that great life, which is the parent of us all, and instead direct our gaze to the small lives that it keeps alive. We call them living and do not see that they cannot live on their own. The real content of the word "living" is "being kept alive."

What, then, is true "living," by its own power? Is it indeed possible for something of this world to be alive of its own accord? Whether to recognize the existence of something beyond the infinite living things, an existence which makes their existence possible, is religion's greatest problem. I have conceived the metaphor of the universe as a human body and our physical existence as a single finger of that body because I believe that it is the universe alone that is truly alive by its own power. The universe is infinite in time and space; since it is also a living organism, its lifespan is infinite, too, without beginning or end. Should we humans, limited in both time and space, wish to believe that our lives are eternal, our only hope is to identify our lives with the life of the universe and unify our physical beings with the great cosmic life.

If the infinite life of the cosmos remains utterly distinct and separate from our lives, religion is impossible, no matter how great the cosmic life is. Yet, as my metaphor of the cosmic body and its finger shows, we are kept alive by the cosmic body; we do not live the lives of our mere physical bodies, but we ourselves are actually living the life of the infinite cosmic body. The finger is not living a finger's life. It lives the same life as the great body of which it is a part.

Here and now we must realize that we are, here and

now, living the great cosmic life and cast off the illusion created by the shortcomings of our physical senses. Since, of course, the cosmic life is the one and only existence, the lives of all people are actually one great life. Your life and my life are not two different lives. All human beings are living the great, infinite life. The only difference is that we perceive that life from slightly different places. It is a matter of a mind appearing in this finger or that finger —that is all. It is not a difference between this body and that body, but of this finger or that finger, and how each feels the life of the same, entire body.

We observed in the previous chapter how our life processes were actually lived on a cosmic scale, and how, if we choose to define our life as restricted to our own small physical body, it is not a life that is lived but a life that is kept alive. Only when we identify our individual existence with the great life that takes place on a cosmic scale are we, for the first time, living a life that is ours. I would like to call this life we live once we identify ourselves with the great cosmic life the True Life. All human beings are living this life, as our bodies are kept alive by it. But while the True Life that we are all living unfolds on a cosmic scale, our minds are restricted to the tiny realm of our individual bodies. The basic contradiction of human existence is here: the gap in scale between the lives we are actually living and the minds we possess. All human sufferings and trials are born of this contradiction. If our lives and our minds were of the same scale and scope, all our problems would disappear. But we cannot hope for this to occur. It is crucial that we fully and clearly understand that the contradiction between our true lives and our minds, which follow the laws of our bodies, the contradiction that is the source of all human pain, is one from which we can never be saved.

The True Life is the only existent life in the cosmos, it alone is living of its own accord, and all other apparently living things are kept alive by it. It is the essential nature of religion to, in this manner, reject from some perspective the idea of the supported existence of individual, finite lives and to establish the notion of a life that lives of its own accord. I would like in the following chapters to investigate the ways in which the three religions of Christianity, Buddhism, and Confucianism accomplish this. But whichever religion we may choose to follow, we must first free ourselves from the illusion that is a product of the origins of the mind before listening to what that religion has to say. Since this illusion has been with us from the very birth of our minds, the awakening from this illusion is, at any rate, our—

          ✍   ✍   ✍

Here the original manuscript breaks off. Everything up to this point was written thirty-four or thirty-five years ago, when I was in my thirties. For all those years this little tract slept in a corner of my bookshelf. When it finally came to my attention, I found it thus, ending incomplete in the middle of chapter 3. I have no idea what happened to the rest.

Now I put my hand to writing the remainder of *A Materialist's Religion*. In the intervening years I have said nothing of this to anyone. It remained locked in my heart, my private view of life. And, in that time, I have changed from a youth who had just risen from his sickbed and begun to take his first tentative steps into the world to a man in his mid-sixties, at the doorway to old age. Somehow I feel it is my duty to organize once and for all my thoughts on this materialist's religion, a duty I can no longer put off.

So it is that I try to call back my thoughts of long ago and set myself to completing the rest of the chapters of this little book, which contains my heart's sustenance over all these years, my religion for a materialist.

4

The New Testament and
the Materialist's Religion

Most people think that Christianity and the materialist's religion are exact opposites, but it is my belief that the essence of Christianity and the religion for the materialist that I am putting forward share a basic conviction.

At the opening of chapter 1, when I first mentioned Christianity, I wrote that my heart could not accept the words of the New Testament. I must now explain how I gradually came to move closer to the New Testament.

In the spring of my twenty-fourth year, I was forced into a battle with sickness that began with pleurisy and soon developed into pulmonary tuberculosis. Either I would win the battle or lose it; I would live or I would die. That was the grim reality that awaited me. At that time there was no medicine for tuberculosis, and I could not avail myself of such surgical methods as collapsement of the lung or removal of ribs. Instead, I devoted myself to a "natural" method of treatment based on absolute rest, fresh air, and nutrition. I was required to remain absolutely motionless on my back in bed, even to eat and eliminate. This life continued, with the understanding of my family and the devoted care of my mother, for weeks, for months. Our house, where my recuperation was taking place, was located on a small piece of land in front of Takadanobaba Station, wedged between one national railway line and another, private line. Trains ran past both sides of our house almost continuously, and when a freight train thundered down the national railway tracks our house shook as if in an earthquake. When one gazed out the window, a forest of smokestacks from the industrial belt that ran between Takadanobaba and Mejirodai met the eyes. They belched clouds of black smoke, and when the wind blew toward our house I often wondered whether it was possible that anyone could recuperate from pulmonary tuberculosis in a place like this.

One day, after I had been totally immobile for almost eight months, I thought: "Unless I recover soon I will never rise again, but die in this bed. All right then, from today until the end I will begin a life of perfect contemplation, to clear my mind of all thoughts and notions. For though my body has been in a state of complete rest, my mind is far from it. My worrying and fretting has clearly slowed my recovery."

It is difficult to keep the mind free from all thoughts for a long time. After managing to clear my mind of thoughts for a little while, stray thoughts would suddenly leap into my head. In order to chase these thoughts out of my mind, I decided to read the New Testament. I selected several passages from the portions of the New Testament I had already read, and when distracting thoughts were about to enter my mind I would take the New Testament in hand and read one of my passages. After reading several lines, the distracting thoughts would leave me, and I would enter immediately again into concentration free from all thoughts. I decided not to read any book except the New Testament, for the simple reason that its words were the most powerful in driving away my distractions. Thus, except for eating, bathing, and sleeping, my entire time was given over to meditation and the New Testament.

Concentration without thoughts is a state of absolute rest for the mind. Of the three aspects of my natural-recovery method from pulmonary tuberculosis, rest was the most important. The semblance of rest, rest of the body unaccompanied by rest of the mind, did not produce results. I continued my meditation without thoughts, with the help of the New Testament, and my days were spent reaching for the book whenever distracting thoughts disturbed my mental rest.

After one month of this, I began to feel that I was moving in a positive direction, toward recovery. As my body began to win out over the tuberculosis germs, I started to feel a physical sense of fulfillment.

I would like to record here some of the words of Christ that helped me drive away distracting thoughts as I lay in my sickbed.

Be not ye therefore like unto them: for your Father knoweth what things ye have need of, before ye ask him.

After this manner therefore pray ye: Our Father, which art in heaven, Hallowed be thy name.

Give us this day our daily bread.

And forgive us our debts, as we forgive our debtors.

And lead us not into temptation, but deliver us from evil: For thine is the kingdom, and the power, and the glory, for ever. Amen.

For if ye forgive men their trespasses, your Heavenly Father will also forgive you:

But if ye forgive not men their trespasses, neither will your Father forgive your trespasses.

Matthew 6:8–15

THE NEW TESTAMENT 23

Therefore I say unto you, Take no thought for your life, what ye shall eat, or what ye shall drink; nor yet for your body, what ye shall put on. Is not life more than meat, and the body than raiment?

Behold the fowls of the air: for they sow not, neither do they reap, nor gather into barns; yet your Heavenly Father feedeth them. Are ye not much better than they?

Therefore take no thought, saying, What shall we eat? or What shall we drink? or, Wherewithal shall we be clothed?

(For after all these things do the Gentiles seek:) for your Heavenly Father knoweth that ye have need of all these things.

But seek ye first the Kingdom of God, and his righteousness; and all these things shall be added unto you.

Take therefore no thought for the morrow: for the morrow shall take thought for the things of itself. Sufficient unto the day is the evil thereof.

Matthew 6:25–26, 31–34

Judge not, that ye be not judged.

For with what judgement ye judge, ye shall be judged: and with what measure ye mete, it shall be measured to you again.

And why beholdest thou the mote that is in thy brother's eye, but considerest not the beam that is in thine own eye?

Or wilt thou say to thy brother, Let me pull out the mote out of thine eye; and, behold, a beam is in thine own eye?

Thou hypocrite, first cast out the beam out of thine own eye; and then shalt thou see clearly to cast out the mote of thy brother's eye.

Matthew 7:1–5

Ask, and it shall be given you; seek, and ye shall find; knock, and it shall be opened unto you:

For everyone that asketh receiveth; and he that seeketh findeth; and to him that knocketh it shall be opened.

Or what man is there of you, whom if his son ask bread, will he give him a stone?

Or if he ask a fish, will he give him a serpent?

If ye, then, being evil, know how to give good gifts unto your children, how much more shall your Father which is in Heaven give good things to them that ask him?

Therefore all things whatsoever ye would that men should do to you, do you even so unto them: for this is the law and the prophets.

Matthew 7:7–12

But when the Pharisees had heard that he put the Sadducees to silence, they were gathered together.

Then one of them, which was a lawyer, asked him a question, tempting him and saying,

Master, which is the great commandment in the law?

Jesus said unto him, Thou shalt love the Lord thy God with all thy heart, with all thy soul, with all thy mind.

This is the first and great commandment.

And the second is like unto it, Thou shalt love thy neighbour as thyself.

On these two commandments hang all the law and the prophets.

Matthew 22:34–40

Be ye not called Rabbi: for one is your Master, even Christ; and all ye are brethren.

And call no man your father upon the earth; for one is your Father, which is in Heaven.

Neither be ye called masters: for one is your Master, even Christ.

But he that is greatest among you shall be your servant.

And whosoever shall exalt himself shall be abased; and he that shall humble himself shall be exalted.

Matthew 23:8–12

And he lifted up his eyes to his disciples, and said, Blessed be ye poor: for yours is the Kingdom of God.

Blessed are ye that hunger now: for ye shall be filled. Blessed are ye that weep now: for ye shall laugh.

Blessed are ye, when men shall hate you, and when they shall separate you from their company, and shall reproach you, and cast out your name as evil, for the Son of man's sake.

Rejoice ye in that day, and leap for joy: for, behold, your reward is great in heaven: for in the like manner did their fathers unto the prophets.

Luke 6:20–23

But I say unto you which hear, Love your enemies, do good to them which hate you,

Bless them that curse you, and pray for them which despitefully use you.

And unto him that smiteth thee on the one cheek offer also the other; and him that taketh away thy cloak forbid not to take thy coat also.

Give to every man that asketh of thee; and of him that taketh away thy goods ask them not again.

And as ye would that men should do to you, do ye also to them likewise.

For if ye love them which love you, what thank have ye? for sinners also love those that love them.

And if ye do good to them which do good to you, what thank have ye? for sinners also do even the same.

And if ye lend to them of whom ye hope to receive, what thank have ye? for sinners also lend to sinners, to receive as much again.

But love ye your enemies, and do good, and lend, hoping for nothing again; and your reward shall be great, and ye shall be the children of the Highest: for he is kind unto the unthankful and to the evil.

Be ye therefore merciful, as your Father also is merciful.

Judge not, and ye shall not be judged; condemn not, and ye shall not be condemned: forgive, and ye shall be forgiven:

Give, and it shall be given unto you; good measure, pressed down, and shaken together, and running over, shall men give into your bosom. For with the same measure that ye mete withal it shall be measured to you again.

Luke 6:27–38

And when he was demanded of the Pharisees, when the Kingdom of God should come, he answered them and said, the Kingdom of God cometh not with observation:

Neither shall they say, Lo here! or lo, there! for, behold, the Kingdom of God is within you.

Luke 17:20–21

And when Jesus saw that he was very sorrowful, he said, How hardly shall they that have riches enter into the Kingdom of God!

For it is easier for a camel to go through a needle's eye, than for a rich man to enter into the Kingdom of God.

And they that heard it said, Who then can be saved?

And he said, The things which are impossible with men are possible with God.

Then Peter said, Lo, we have left all, and followed thee.

And he said unto them, Verily I say unto you, There is no man that hath left house, or parents, or brethren, or wife, or children, for the Kingdom of God's sake, Who shall not receive manifold more in this present time, and in the world to come life everlasting.

Luke 18:24–30

As I continued my practice of meditation without thoughts, summer arrived. My bed was moved to an open corridor, and since I slept without bedclothes, mosquitoes plagued me. At first I chased them away, but since that distracted me from my rest I gave it up. I let the mosquitoes bite me as they pleased, and sought only to lose myself in my meditation.

After two months of this practice, I was told by my doctor, "It's about time for you to try to raise your upper body up in bed." But, thinking that it was best not to rush things, I continued to observe absolute rest for a bit longer. Then, halfway through the summer came a day that I will never forget. It was exactly one year from the day I came down with a high fever and began my life of absolute bed rest. The feeling that unexpectedly passed through my mind on that day was this: "I have lived a life of absolute bed rest for one full year now. I have only lived this long thanks to the devoted nursing of my mother; I don't have the power to keep myself alive. Flat on my back in bed for a year, I would be better described as being kept alive than as living.

"Yes, that's it. And who made the food that my mother brings to my pillow for me to eat? Who carried it all the long way to Tokyo? All of these people, those who grew the food and those who transported it, to all of them I owe my very life. I am kept alive not only by my mother and father, my family, but by all those many, many people working day and night. Yes, I am kept alive, I am given life. How grateful I am. I thank, from the bottom of my heart, all those numberless, nameless people who are keeping me alive."

My heart was full to brimming with gratitude and relief, and, at the same time, a spring of great joy bubbled up from the depths of my heart.

Though I remained prone on my bed as before, once I realized that I was being kept alive by the efforts of all those around me, once I felt that gratitude and joy, all of the dissatisfactions that had troubled my heart before disappeared.

The freight trains that rumbled past shaking the house at night like an earthquake were no longer the enemies of my rest, but the friends who brought my sustenance to me. Even the factory smokestacks belching their black clouds were my life's benefactors. I decided to be thankful for the efforts of these former enemies. And when I had this awakening to the fact that I was being kept alive by all around me, I decided, after a year of complete rest, to begin to practice raising my upper body from the bed.

With the help of my mother I was able to sit up for five minutes. My convalescence continued for another eight years, but it was on that one-year anniversary that I began a new life, in both body and mind.

I continued to read the New Testament after that, and

I found myself aware of a meaning to Christ's words that I had not felt up to that time. Up to just the day before, I had only read the words of the New Testament because of their strange power to dispel my disturbing and distracting thoughts. But reading them after my awakening I immediately felt that these were not words from the mind of a man, but a call to us from that "Great Life" which keeps us all alive.

Christ's teachings to "love God with all thy heart, with all thy soul, with all thy mind," and "to love thy neighbor as thyself" could not possibly be words from the mind of self-centered man. When I first realized that I was being kept alive, I could not help but also affirm the existence of some "Great Life" (I had no other way to describe it) that also kept all other human beings alive. And when I read Christ's words, replacing "God" with this "Great Life" that I had felt, each and every word of his teachings penetrated to the very core of my heart.

If the Great Life I speak of does possess a heart, a mind, an intelligence, before that intelligence there is no distinction between "self" and "other," as humans feel it. The intelligence that says "Love thy neighbor as thyself" can be no other intelligence than that of the Great Life.

Perhaps it is because the words of Christ come from the intelligence of the Great Life that they are so hard for men to understand with their small minds. The mind that man is born with is an egocentric mind, and it is only natural that the egocentric mind cannot understand words that spring from the intelligence of the Great Life.

To say that in the intelligence of the Great Life there is neither self nor others is to say, in our human words, that self and others are one. To say that they are one is to say that both are kept alive by the Great Life, and that, even in material terms, one cannot be separated from the other. The belief that the self and others are separate entities is merely the assumption of the egocentric mind, an illusion of the human mind, blind to the real activities of life around it.

Many religious writings speak of "the identity of self and others"; I understand it in the fashion described above. And Christianity as well teaches the identity of self and others using a variety of expressions. "The Highest . . . is kind unto the unthankful and to the evil.

"Be ye therefore merciful, as your Father also is merciful" (Luke 6:35–36).

5

The Core of
the Buddha's Teaching

Buddhism is made up of many different schools, each with their characteristic doctrines and methods (*upaya,* "skill-in-means"). These are profound and difficult to understand, and I do not pretend to be an expert on any of them; still, I would like to set forth here my own personal reconciliation of some of Buddhism's major teachings, for though vastly different in appearance and emphasis, I believe that there is certainly an essential core shared by all sects. For whatever shortcomings my analysis of these difficult topics may contain, I beg the reader's pardon, and can offer as my only excuse that my fragmentary knowledge of the Buddha's teachings is not that of a philosopher, but of a seeker.

Perhaps the farthest poles of Japanese Buddhism are represented by the Pure Land school (Jodo shu) and the Zen school (Zen shu). The Pure Land sect teaches that its believers will be reborn in the Pure Land of the West by giving themselves over completely to what they call "other-power"—the power of the Buddha Amida. The Zen school, on the other hand, emphasizes that enlightenment—which they call satori—is only to be achieved through one's own power, one's diligent, relentless quest. I do not know whether Shakyamuni Buddha taught both "self-power" and "other-power" or whether the difficulty of the Buddha's original teachings prompted his later followers to adopt these approaches as devices to aid later Buddhists in their practice. But what I am convinced of is that these two apparently opposite approaches spring from a common, all-encompassing ground; and that is what I wish to explore in this chapter.

We must expand the discussion to include not only these two sects of Japanese Buddhism, but a third and very important school of Buddhism that flourishes in Japan: the Nichiren sect, named after its founder, Nichiren (1222–82). The main teaching of Nichiren and his followers is that the true teaching of the Buddha is transmitted in the *Lotus Sutra,* one of the most important Buddhist texts in East Asia. Finally, the thoughts of the Japanese philosopher Kitaro Nishida (1870–1945) will also shed light on our search. Nishida is best known for his attempt to incorporate basic principles of Buddhist thought within the tradition of Western speculative thought in order to create a new Eastern Philosophy.

What, then, is the all-encompassing ground that is the source and support of not only the teachings of the various Buddhist sects, but the principles of Nishida's new Eastern Philosophy? I believe it to be the principle that all human beings exist by virtue of the Buddha, and that all life can be ultimately reduced to the Buddha. Likewise, all causes and effects are bound together in such a way that all phenomena are ultimately identical in both cause and effect. This is a rather difficult proposition, so let us break it into its components and discuss them one by one.

The first truth is that all human life—indeed, all life— is from Buddha and returns to Buddha. How is this truth embodied in the major schools of Japanese Buddhism? According to the "other-power" Buddhism founded and propagated by Honen (1133–1212) and Shinran (1173–1262), one only has to single-mindedly invoke the name of Amida Buddha and to take refuge in him in order to be assured of birth in his Pure Land. Since enlightenment is forever beyond the reach of the one who relies on his own meagre powers of discriminative reason, this is man's best and only course. Though approaching the problem from a different direction, the "self-power" Zen school offers a message remarkably similar: it urges us to apply ourselves in *zazen* in order to awaken to *mu* ("nothingness"), or, as Zen master Dogen (1200–53) instructed, to "throw off both body and mind." Both of these phrases instruct us to abandon the claims of the ego.

The Nichiren sect teaches, as I mentioned earlier, that the *Lotus Sutra* is the Buddha's true teaching. But what part of the *Lotus Sutra* is the core of its truth? I am inclined to believe that the famous passage "the ultimate identity of the origins and ends [of all existence]" is that core. This is actually the conclusion of a crucial section in the "Skill-in-Means" chapter of the sutra, which reads: "Only a Buddha and a Buddha can know the reality of the elements of existence (dharmas), that is, the suchness of their characteristics, the suchness of their nature, the suchness of their substance, the suchness of their powers, the suchness of their functions, the suchness of their causes, the suchness of their conditions, the suchness of their effects, the suchness of their retributions, and the ultimate identity of their origins and ends." This pivotal passage is known as the "ten suchnesses" (*ju nyoze*), and is traditionally regarded as the philosophical core of the *Lotus Sutra*. It means, in effect, that all the things of this world, in various shapes and forms, with various natures, substances, powers, and activities, serve as causes which, combining with certain conditions, produce many different results, that in turn engender other responses in the world—yet all of these phenomena are expressions of one universal principle, and from start to finish are essentially alike and equal. This, then, is Buddha: this eternal, unchanging, all-encompassing universal truth which is, at the same time, the source of the myriad phenomena of our world.

Once we have truly grasped "the ten suchnesses," it almost seems as if Shakyamuni Buddha were aware of that discovery of modern physics, the Law of the Conservation of Matter. It is when we apply this general principle to our own lives that we become aware of the truth of the statement that human life—all life—is from Buddha and returns to Buddha. Thus the "other-power" Buddhism that teaches single-mindedly invoking the name of Amida and seeking salvation in unconditional faith, as well as the Buddhism that seeks to awaken to *mu* and to "throw off the body and the mind" in Zen meditation, are both based on the universal truth of the ultimate equality, from start to finish, of all phenomena.

Let us now move on to the second half of our proposition: that all causes and effects are bound together as one, and that all things in the world have only one true cause and effect. The last five of the ten suchnesses are "the suchness of their causes, the suchness of their conditions, the suchness of their effects, the suchness of their retributions," and the conclusion, "the ultimate identity of their origins and their ends." This emphasis on actions and their results shows why Buddhism is often regarded as a philosophy of cause and effect, or karma. The philosopher Kitaro Nishida focused on this aspect of Buddhism in the creation of his complex and difficult philosophical system. Nishida rephrases the Buddhist doctrine of karma as follows: "The created thing creates the creating thing." In Buddhist terminology, "the created thing" is the effect; "the creating thing" is the cause. In other words, effect is not simply effect, but also becomes a cause, and, further, the cause of yet another cause. Thus cause becomes effect and effect becomes cause in an endless chain in which it is impossible to positively identify any exclusive cause or effect. Like a spider's web, like the interstices of a net, cause and effect mutually create each other and become one in substance. This is, in fact, "the ultimate identity of origins and ends" that the *Lotus Sutra* speaks of, and when we penetrate the true relationship between cause and effect, we see that there is only one cause and one effect in all the universe.

If we apply this once again to our own lives, we see that people are all created things. Whether good or evil, all men and women are merely created things, and any talk of praise or blame is meaningless, since we are not our own products. But there is more to our existence than this, for we also "create creating things." Our every blink and nod serves as a cause that influences the creation of our surroundings. Nor does the influence of our activity stop there, for it goes on to become yet another cause that will produce a further cause. From this point of view, every person is tremendously responsible for his each and every thought and action. We bear the responsibility not only to improve the lot of those around us, but also to improve our own.

The *Jataka* tales, the ancient collection of stories telling of the lives of the Buddha before he attained enlightenment, contain a tale that beautifully illuminates our topic. The Bodhisattva (literally, "being who seeks wisdom"; for that is what the Buddha was known as before he was enlightened) was engaged in austerities in the mountain wilderness when suddenly, from somewhere, he heard a sonorous voice intoning the verse: "All existence is impermanent, this is the fact of birth and death." When the Bodhisattva looked up to see the source of the voice, he found himself confronted with a horrible demon. "Did you intone the verse I just heard? Please, I beg you, teach me its conclusion!" pleaded the Bodhisattva. "I will do that on one condition," replied the demon, "and that is that after you have heard it, you throw yourself from the cliff on which you are perched. If you are prepared to die, I will tell you the final refrain."

"If I can only hear this verse and attain enlightenment, I am prepared to die immediately." And thus the demon intoned the final lines: "Put an end to birth and death, and take nirvana as your joy." Hearing these words, the Bodhisattva was enlightened in an instant, and said to the demon: "My greatest thanks. Thanks to you I have been enlightened. I die now without the slightest regret." And, in accord with his promise, he threw himself off the cliff. But as he plummeted from his mountain perch, his fall was suddenly stopped and he was held in the air as if by a giant hand. He looked to see that the demon of moments before had been transformed into the god Indra, and he was holding the Bodhisattva tenderly in his palm.

The *Jatakas* proclaims that the deepest truth of Buddhism only revealed itself to the Bodhisattva when he had a decided to sacrifice his own life to attain it.

But the final lines of the quatrain, "Put an end to birth and death, and take nirvana as your joy," are difficult for us to fathom, partly because such terms as "birth and death" and nirvana are radically different from the concepts we are familiar with in our daily lives. "Birth and death" refers to our conventional world of things and activities, the first nine of the ten suchnesses, the world of change and impermanence. Nirvana, on the other hand, refers to the last of the ten suchnesses, "the ultimate identity of origins and ends." In this universal principle there are no changes, no activities, no individuals—all is equal and eternal. Indra's verse tells the Bodhisattva to abandon the world of the impermanent for the bliss of nirvana.

What we must not overlook is that the parable so eloquently insists a "leap" is necessary to transform the mind of birth and death to the mind of nirvana. The Bodhisattva throws himself from the cliff into the abyss. The Zen school, in a remarkable parallel, asks the practitioner to "throw off" his mind and body. Certainly, without this throwing off it is impossible to discover the eternally equal, unchanging realm, the nirvana behind our world of impermanence.

One of the most familiar sutras to Japanese Buddhists is the *Heart Sutra* (*Hannya Shin Gyo*), which contains the hallowed verse: "Form is emptiness and emptiness is form." From yet another perspective, this sutra delivers the same message as the ten suchnesses and the *Jataka* tale related above. "Form" includes the first nine suchnesses, all of the distinguishing features of distinct phenomena as they appear in the world; "emptiness," of course, is the famous sunyata, Buddhism's key concept: it is equivalent to the last of the suchnesses, the ultimate identity of all phenomena. "Emptiness" in Buddhism does not refer to a vacuum of any sort; it is, rather, the lack of any substantial substratum in individual existents. Just because all things are empty, they are "unchanging from start to finish, always equal"—the tenth suchness. The *mu* (which we previously translated as nothingness) of the Zen school is actually this very special Buddhist emptiness. And since the fundamental teaching of the Zen school is to throw off the mind and body and awaken to *mu*, it seeks no different end than that taught in the *Lotus Sutra*.

Let us now consider this "throwing off the mind and body" a bit more closely. I wish to show that the story of the Bodhisattva's enlightenment when he threw himself from the cliff to hear the verse "Put an end to birth and death, and take nirvana as your joy" is no different from throwing off the mind and body to realize for the first time that beyond this world where all things are impermanent there lies a great universal truth. But what does "throwing off the body and mind" mean, actually? In the parable, the Bodhisattva threw himself from the cliff; but we must understand this metaphor in terms of the human mind, of course. In other words, the Bodhisattva's act of throwing himself into the precipice stands for our spiritual act of throwing away our notion of self. As long as we regard the phenomena of the world from the standpoint of the self, they remain impermanent, they remain bound to the world of birth and death. They are utterly divorced from the universal principle of equality and eternity, and can only be felt as the continually changing world of existence.

The notion of self is opposed to the notion of others. Our minds adopt this notion from a very early stage, and when told to abandon the self, we are faced with considerable difficulty. First of all, we cannot separate ourselves from our bodies. When we think of something, it is our brain that is doing the thinking. In fact, it is ultimately impossible to divorce ourselves entirely from the notion of self. Faced with this reality, we can only feel despair, for enlightenment as to the ultimate truths of the universe is impossible for our human minds. Zen attempts to break through this barrier with the "self-power" method of meditation, while Pure Land Buddhism surrenders all efforts and teaches that the only method is to invoke the Buddha's name. But both begin from the fervent wish to somehow free ourselves from the chains of self that bind us; both are attempts to find a place of peace and rest for the hearts of men, weary of the suffering that is always attendant in the world of impermanence.

Perhaps we can never completely "throw off the body and the mind," but must continue to pursue this goal, must continue to make our way toward this far shore of enlightenment, for eternity. Though we know we will never reach it, the human heart is weak; it cannot bear to give up the pursuit, it cannot bear to live without hope.

This is a quality we all share, and it is the reason that most people reach a point when they must search out a faith, a religion.

The essential core of Buddhism is, for me, the Buddha. And the Buddha is the very principle we have spoken of so many times, the ultimate unchanging equality of all phenomena, empty, still, eternal, that yet produces all the myriad phenomena of the world, in their infinite variety. It is for that reason that I say we are all given life by the Buddha, who is the sole parent of all human life. We humans tend to believe that this body is our self, and that we are living by means of our own power. But this is merely the self's thin illusion. Reflection shows that we do not live by our own power, but are given life. If we compare the Buddha in his entirety to a person, each of us, as an individual, would be no more than one finger on his hand. Of course the finger has no separate existence, yet, if it had a mind, it would surely think that it did exist entirely by virtue of itself. Our conviction that we have a separate existence is just as mistaken. Our minds are nothing more than a finger's mind: a limited phenomenon with illusions of grandeur. Yet should that odd little "finger-mind" realize somehow that it was not simply one finger that was living, that instead the finger was a part of a much greater existence which gave it life, and, in fact, that the greater existence was identical to the little finger's existence, it would surely rejoice.

In closing, I would like to consider the word *magokoro* for a moment. *Magokoro* means, literally, "true heart"; it is often translated as sincerity, but probably no single English word quite shares its general range and specific nuance. Perhaps "altruism" comes closest, but it lacks the colloquial ring of the original. In Japanese it is often said "That person is true-hearted," or "His actions are always true-hearted." Yet what exactly is this heart, this mind (for they are synonymous in Japanese), that is said to be true? A little reflection shows that we use the term to describe a person who cares as much for others as for himself, who does things for others as willingly as if it were for himself. Perhaps we can define "true-heartedness," then, as "the mind of the identity of self and others." There are people who seem to behave altruistically as if by nature. Though they may not subscribe to any particular religion, they surely possess the mind of the Buddha.

It is as defined above that I will use the term "true-heartedness" in my religion for materialists. We will discuss it in greater detail in the seventh chapter. Here let it suffice us to say that the true heart is one that partakes of true life. This true life is not the life of one finger, but the greater life that gives life to us all. Release from the notion of the individual self and awakening to the greater self of the universe is what is meant by throwing away the mind and body. Finally, when the body and mind are discarded, the bliss of nirvana is reached.

6

Our True Body

The *Caigen Tan* is a work by Hong Zicheng of the Ming dynasty (1368–1644). In this work, Hong has distilled the essences of Confucianism, Buddhism, and Taoism. In addition, he gives detailed accounts of the vagaries of the world and human affairs, all presented in a sophisticated and polished literary style. In short, his masterpiece is an unexcelled handbook for life.

I would like to select several passages from among the many of the *Caigen Tan* that present the core truth of Confucianism, Buddhism, and Taoism, and record them here.

> Hearing the sound of a bell on
>   a quiet night
> I awake from my dream within a dream
> And gaze at the floating reflection
>   of the moon
> To see the body outside the body.

This short verse is perhaps the pithiest expression of the idea of the identity of self and others that permeates the *Caigen Tan*. What does it mean? I think that the reflection of the moon floating on one of the small ripples in the pond is my self. Perhaps the moon shining on the next little ripple is you. There is only one moon, yet the pond is alive with infinite reflections of it. Each and every one of those infinite reflections dancing on the ripples is the light of the same, single moon. In the same fashion that the true being of each tiny moon reflection is the light of the great moon in the heavens, my true self is not this tiny physical body, but the great life force of the universe that gives me, and all of us, life.

As illusory manifestations, virtue, fame, wealth, and honor, and indeed this very body are only temporary forms; in their true state, parents and siblings and indeed all things are one in substance. The person who is able to see, to recognize, and to attain the realm of truth, will be able to carry the empire on his shoulders and free himself from the chains of the world.

Awakening to the "illusory manifestations," in other words becoming aware of the impermanent nature of the world, and understanding the true nature of the universe—"the realm of truth"—are inconceivable as separate achievements. To rephrase this idea, it is impossible to awaken to the truth of impermanence as long as one clings to ego; yet unless one can awaken to that truth, it is very difficult to understand the true nature of the universe. Human beings are born with egos and go through their lives with egos, and that is why it is so very difficult for them to awaken to such ideas as "impermanence" and "the realm of truth." When we consider the process of the formation of the human mind and trace it to its source, it is hardly surprising that the ego is such an adamantine, stubborn thing.

In order to grasp such concepts as impermanence and the realm of truth we must consider the question What is it that is truly alive? And in order to understand the teachings of the *Caigen Tan* it is necessary, I am convinced, to have awakened to the fact that we are given life, and that the thing which gives us life is that which is truly alive. This "truly alive" existence is the identity of all things and myself, the realization that self and others are one.

The people of the world believe the self truly exists, and thus are born all sorts of preferences, all sorts of sufferings. An ancient sage said, "Since I don't know that I possess a self, how can I regard things as valuable?" And he also said, "Since I know this body is not the self, where can sufferings attack me?" These words are words of truth indeed.

This passage of the *Caigen Tan* is one that expresses the idea of escape from the self in especially strong and clear terms. The self is, of course, the ego. This verse asks us to try to escape from a self-centered way of thinking, to abandon the small self and to know the Great Self. For we are likely to take the tiny reflection of the moon on the pond's momentary ripple as our self—and a small self it is. Only when we realize that the source of the countless tiny moon reflections is the great moon in the sky are we able to know the Great Self, the Great Life of the universe that is the parent of the life that dwells, like a reflection, in our tiny physical bodies.

7

The Seed of the True Mind

Man is the lord of all creation, it is said. Man is more intelligent than any other animal. He has created an advanced culture. Spiritually and emotionally, too, he is advanced; he experiences emotions and feelings that other animals cannot, and possesses such powers of thought that he has created philosophy and religion. It is certainly fitting, then, to regard him as the lord of all creation.

The True Mind that we discussed in chapter 5, too, (there we called it "true-heartedness") is without a doubt the exclusive possession of man. Occasionally it seems as if the love that other animals show their offspring surpasses that of human parents, but this "love" is the product of instinct, and we should probably consider it a phenomenon distinct from the True Mind with which we are concerned.

What is the essence of the True Mind? What is its source? These are the questions I addressed myself to. All of us human beings are comrades, short-lived individuals given life by a far greater life. This is the undeniable reality, whether we realize it or not. It is this reality that, at the bottom of the human heart, instinctively, makes us aware of the fact that we are all brothers given life by the same source. This, I believe, is the origin of the True Mind:

the Great Life that gives us all life is the source of the True Mind. I call the essence of the True Mind, which resides in the unconscious depths of the human heart, the True Mind. And, since the True Mind flows out from the Great Life, I call that life the True Life.

The True Body is, of course, the universe itself. And you and I are each but one finger of that great, universal body.

8

The True Practice

I think it can be said that the everyday actions of men are almost entirely governed by the physical mind. I have spoken in earlier chapters about the fact that our physical minds are like the mind of a single finger of the body of true existence. So powerfully does the physical mind control us that, perhaps, rather than regarding our minds as occupied by the "one-finger mind," it is more appropriate to say that the one-finger mind is, in fact, the human mind.

Yet, at the bottom of the human unconscious, the True Mind dwells. This is a natural result of the fact that we are given life by the True Life; it is only that the physical mind remains unaware of this fact. The True Mind lies buried beneath the everyday, physical mind, which is not even aware of its existence.

And so it is that the physcial mind usually occupies the greater part of our consciousness, and appears to be wide-ranging and extremely strong. Yet when a person meets with adversity, the physical mind immediately reveals its true character, and its control wobbles. At such times, the physical mind changes suddenly and all its weaknesses come to the fore, showing what an extremely undependable thing it is. And at such times the True Mind, long hidden in the depths of the unconscious, lifts its head and extends a helping hand to us.

At such times, the True Mind dwelling in the weak human body faces its parent, the True Life, and raises its voice in prayer. When the physical mind finds itself powerless, the first thing that the True Mind does is to pray. When at last its time comes and the True Mind awakens, it prays with all its might, in search of the love of its parent.

Zen master Dogen taught the Zen meditation of "just sitting" (*shikan daza*). For Dogen, this was the ultimate practice, and he taught that enlightenment was to be found in it. "Just sitting" was, for him, not a means to enlightenment, but enlightenment itself. The reason, according to Dogen, that the practice of "just sitting" is the realm of enlightenment itself, is that this practice was the "practice of the one suchness" (*ichinyo no gyo*). What sort of practice could this be? To put it simply, it is "the practice in which self and object are melded into one." Perhaps we could also call it a practice in which the self is forgotten—at any rate, it is not a practice that is carried out by the self. For Dogen this was "just sitting," and just sitting was enlightenment itself.

Because of the rest I found in the state of no thoughts, my illness took a turn toward recovery, and for the first time in a year I was able to sit up in my bed. After that I gradually began to gain strength, and soon I was able to walk about my room, and even, later, outside the house. Then, one day, just as I was beginning to entertain hopes of recovery, I was struck by a second terrible blow.

I felt an odd sort of irritation in my throat. When I examined it in the mirror, I saw against the red of my throat lining a single tiny white spot. For several days I continued to observe the spot. Sometimes, unawares, it would disappear; but then the next day the same white spot would be there, in a slightly different location. I was overwhelmed by a sinking feeling of despair. Tuberculosis of the larynx. Incurable tuberculosis of the larynx. My mind became prey to terrible uncertainty as I began to think that the white spot in my own throat was the first sign of the disease.

The probability of tuberculosis of the larynx occurred to me because, as I began to recover and regain strength, the amount of phlegm that I coughed up had begun to increase. It was difficult to completely clear my throat of this infected phlegm, and I was forced to cough with considerable force to do so. Since I was ridding my body of an infected fluid, and since it was only the increase in my strength that allowed me to cough up the phlegm, I took it as a reassuring sign of my recovery, and was glad for it. Yet I also knew that the sound of my coughing was not a pleasant one for those around me, and so I would hold the phlegm in my throat, bearing the discomfort, until one of the trains that ran by our house passed. With the rumbling of the trains masking the sound, I could cough up the fluid with the great heaving coughs that were necessary. It would have been only too easy for the bacteria from the infected phlegm that I held in my throat to attach themselves to its lining and begin to incubate there.

But I only realized this too late, and there was nothing I could do about it now. After my lungs were finally on the way to recovery, I had contracted tuberculosis of the larynx—and my reading on the subject had all confirmed that it was an incurable variety of the disease. The natural conclusion was that all I could do was to prepare to die.

I spoke of this to no one. Though I had my doctor look at the white spot in my throat, he said nothing, and I dared not pursue the subject with him.

After spending several painful days worrying about this alone, I decided to go to the seashore. After the New Year's holidays, I left, led by my mother, on a Tokai Line steamship bound for Shimoda. At the time, I thought I would never see my home again. It was with that resolution that I left it. My destination was a quiet little inn called the Shinguya in Kakizaki, facing Shimoda Bay. The Shinguya operated as both a shipping agent and an inn at that time, and also offered long-term lodgings to people like me, who went there for rest and recovery. The lively old couple who owned the inn recounted how they had moved here from Shingu in Kishu to the south, and named their new inn after their native place. Their son worked at the local government offices, and their daughter-in-law was in handy charge of the inn's kitchen. The young couple was blessed with five daughters of their own.

I soon felt as if I were a member of the family myself. Another patient recovering from tuberculosis, a fellow about my age named Sato, was staying at the Shinguya as well. On several occasions Sato and I took photos of the little girls and presented them to their mother. The next day she would inevitably offer us some special treat and be extra kind to us.

I actually began to enjoy this life by the sea, and somehow evaded the terror of tuberculosis of the larynx that had once gripped me. As before, I spent the better part of each day in bed, devoted to my practice of meditation without thoughts. The young mistress of the inn once asked me if I wasn't terribly bored. I answered in all sincerity that I was least bored when engaged in my meditation. Sato wryly remarked that I was certainly the philosophical type, and used to laugh about it.

I stayed at the Shinguya for some three months, and all during that time I lived with the knowledge that my disease might progress gradually and I might have to confront death. I even contemplated just how I would die when the time came. Soon Shimoda Bay left winter behind and turned toward spring, and the time for the seaweed harvest arrived. It was just at this time, when the waters of the bay before the inn were afloat with little boats gathering *wakame,* that I happened to open a copy of the magazine *Natural Healing* (*Ryoyo Seikatsu*) that had been sent to me. My gaze fell from the school of bobbing boats to the cover of the magazine, where I saw the words "Special Issue on Tuberculosis of the Larynx."

The issue included several case histories of the disease. Doctor Toshizo Daito, the head of the ears, nose, and throat department of Nihon Ika Daigaku (Japan Medical College), contributed an article in which he commented on each of these case histories and discussed the disease. I read the issue greedily and was quickly made to realize just how little I had really known about tuberculosis of the larynx. One of Dr. Daito's remarks, in particular, struck home: "Though it is not the case in any of the histories printed here, there is a form of tuberculosis of the larynx in which all symptoms go undetected by the patient."

I immediately decided to return to Tokyo, and sent a telegram home to that effect. My mother met me at the dock in Tokyo, and I returned home—something I had never thought I would do only three months before.

The very next day I went to the Nihon Ika Daigaku hospital and was examined by Dr. Daito, who was all encouragement. He assured me that as my tuberculosis was cured and I gained strength, the tuberculosis of the larynx would also be cured. He confirmed that I was indeed recovering from the first disease, and urged me to have confidence in my fight with the illness. He also advised me to rest my throat as much as possible. I was immensely grateful for his kindness, and, while deeply regretting the worry I had put myself through because of my own ignorance, concluded that Heaven had not yet abandoned me. It was with great joy that I returned home that day.

The next day I invited my elder brother to a nearby coffee shop and told him everything that had passed until now. I explained to him that I wished to begin my fight with the disease by following Dr. Daito's suggestion to rest my throat completely by refraining totally from speech. I asked for his consent and his help.

And so my life of silence began. I communicated with my family by written notes, but I didn't explain the reason to my parents because I didn't wish to worry them unnecessarily.

I cannot recall precisely how long I continued this life of silence, but I believe it was about six months. At any rate, after a period of complete rest for my throat the white spot no longer appeared and the strange feeling in my throat was gone and forgotten.

From the time I had first discovered the white spot on my throat lining until the day Dr. Daito examined me, I had lived daily with the presence of death. And as I battled with the fear of my own imminent death I also continued to contemplate ways in which man might triumph over that fear. My conclusion was that mankind transcends the realm of birth and death through practice. It is impossible to find any transcendental enlightenment outside the realm of our practice. From birth, all men have achieved transcendence of the realm of birth and death through practice. Normally, our lives are pleasant enough; but it is a mistake, when we come up against some obstacle, to fall away from our practice and begin to contemplate how the fear of death may be conquered. I realized that it was when I was doing something, when I had forgotten everything in my practice, that I was alive and able to forget completely about both life and death.

Our practice begins when we are born and continues until we die. This is what it is to be a human being. The human life through which runs the constant thread of practice is the life that has transcended birth and death.

Earlier I spoke of Master Dogen's practice as the practice of the one suchness, and explained that the one suchness is the melding of subject and object into one through activity. I also described Dogen's teaching of discarding the body and the mind as concentrating one's entire body and mind on one object, in which one becomes lost. Forgetting oneself and giving oneself entirely to the object or activity, this selflessness, this forgetting, that is Dogen's teaching. Since, as I concluded, all men have from birth transcended birth and death through their practice, it seems that we are all natural experts at Dogen's practice of discarding the body and the mind.

But I'd like to dig a bit deeper into the meaning of practice. For although mankind may be naturally expert at Dogen's discarding the body and the mind, I think there is still much that we need to consider. There are many different types of practice, first of all. Practice can be motivated by desire, by responsibility, by interest, by service, and by many other different impulses. Yet whatever sort of practice it is, in it we can achieve the transcendence of the realm of birth and death.

Nevertheless, there are times when the differences among these practices make themselves apparent. The practice motivated by desire, for example, is overturned and loses its base when the problem of our own life and death is brought before our eyes. On the other hand, the practice motivated by responsibility is not challenged by the problems of life and death. I wish to learn a firm and unwavering practice that will serve me at any time, in any event, and that will never desert me. The practice of the single-finger mind is easily destroyed, but the practice of the True Mind is strong. It is my daily effort to move from the practice of the small self to the practice of the Great Self.

9

The Mind's Evolution

I wish to avoid a conclusion that either materialism or mentalism is correct. Our human intelligence is of an extremely limited scope, and it is impossible to completely understand with it anything as great as the universe itself. Whichever may be closer to the truth, it was as a materialist that, more than thirty years ago, I began to think about religion. Actually, it is more accurate to say that I was driven to think about religion by unavoidable circumstances.

I bring this small tract to a close with a sentence from a letter I wrote at that time to an honored friend, an acquaintance of my school days whose advice helped me through my difficult recovery, and who had himself battled tuberculosis. He wrote me while I was keeping total silence in an attempt to heal my throat, inquiring about my state of mind; and I replied to him:

> There is nothing more to life than doing what must be done, finishing what must be finished. From a personal point of view, there is success and failure in life. But once we have abandoned the small self and awakened to the Great Self, we see that all is nothing but the evolving development of the Buddha.

Postscript

After completing the Preface of this work, I visited Dr. Fumio Masutani. I had quoted freely from him in that portion of my book, and I wished to seek his permission to reproduce his words before publication. The day I first met Dr. Masutani, he was busy inspecting the proofs of the second volume of his four-volume translation from the Pali of the *Nikayas;* the first volume had just come out a few days before. In spite of the task that engaged him, he was kind enough to meet me, and even went so far as to instruct me on certain questions that I had. Finally he reached up to a nearby shelf and, taking down a copy of his *Shakuson no Satori* (The Buddha's Enlightenment), signed it and presented it to me. At that time he mentioned to me that Mr. Niwano, the leader of the lay-Buddhist organization Rissho Kosei Kai, had asked to meet with him to learn more of early Buddhism. Dr. Masutani volunteered that Rissho Kosei Kai was publishing some fine books on Buddhism as well.

I thanked Dr. Masutani profusely and read his book all the way home. Immediately after arriving there, I found the copy of *Bukkyo no Hongi* (The Essential Truth of Buddhism) published by Kosei Shuppansha that had been tucked away in a corner of my bookshelf and opened it. I saw that the book was divided into three sections, the first on the essentials of early Buddhism, the second on the fundamental truths of Buddhism as seen from the point of view of the *Lotus Sutra* literature, and the third on practice and activity based on Buddhist principles. A closer look at the table of contents showed that the intent of the book was the very reconciliation of early Buddhism and Mahayana Buddhism that Dr. Masutani advocated.

I would like to quote several passages from that work below. Since I touched upon the first part of the book in my Preface, I will restrict myself to the latter two parts here. There are many fine passages of great truth throughout the book, but in particular I was impressed with what was written in the second part—the clear presentation of the spirit of the *Lotus Sutra* in chapter 4, "*Muryogikyo no Yotai*" (The Basic Truths of the *Sutra of Innumerable Meanings*). The following passages are from that chapter.

What are the true characteristics? When we speak of "content" we mean the things that we see with our eyes, hear with our ears, touch with our hands—the world of phenomena. This world appears to be varied and complex, constantly changing and moving, but the true characteristics behind that surface are eternal and always preserve a great harmony as they pass through their changes.

Most people find this hard to grasp. That is not without reason, either. The things now before your eyes, the book, the desk, the ink, the glass, the water in it, are all individual things and all seem to exist in definite shapes. It is impossible to believe that they are originally all the same.

But modern science has in fact already proven that they are the same. According to nuclear physics, all matter is composed of protons, neutrons, electrons, and other particles. The apparent differences in objects are the result of different combinations of those basic particles. . . .

Nuclear physicists are now in search of the source of the thirty-some types of atomic particles they have identified. Whether it be called emptiness, ultimate matter, or energy, they are certain that it is an invisible, untouchable, vague, and uniform in its existence. . . .

We have proof as well that the particles which make up matter do not move about purely at whim. Under certain conditions they come together in defined patterns to form elements such as uranium, gold, hydrogen, and oxygen. What is it, then, that creates those conditions? That is still unknown.

Great religious leaders such as the Buddha have been able to see directly with their insight the existence of the power which creates those conditions. They have discovered—and tried to teach somehow us ordinary men, in terms we can understand—the Great Life, the truth, the great original power, the world of true existence behind the world of phenomena, which makes everything exist, gives everything life and movement.

This world of true existence has also been seen directly by some of the most brilliant of modern scientists. The two examples given below have been quoted often before, but since they are the proclamations of two giants of the world of science, they deserve repeating here.

Albert Einstein: ". . . I know that a certain something that we cannot fully describe truly exists, and I know that it is the supreme intelligence and of blinding beauty. And I know that with my poor intelligence I can only perceive the fringe of the fringe. This awareness, this emotion, is the core of the true religious spirit."

Dr. Hideki Yukawa: "Present reality is hard. It excludes any softness. Suddenly it changes in unexpected ways. All balances are destroyed, sooner or later. Present reality is complex. Hasty conclusions are taboo. In spite of all this, present reality always moves following a single law that is found in its depths. Only a superior man can divine it. Yet present reality is always in harmony with the law that is its base. Only the poets can discover it.

"Superior men are rare, poets are rare. The rest of us ordinary people always tend somehow to get too bound up in present reality. Thus it is that we change suddenly like that reality, we grow complicated as that reality, we end up as uncertain as that reality. And we fail to recognize the greater world of true reality that dwells behind the present reality.

"Don't ask where in present reality to find true reality. True reality will become present reality soon enough."

Four of Dr. Yukawa's statements seem as if they were written precisely for the task of explaining this *Muryogikyo* (*Sutra of Innumerable Meanings*): "Present reality always moves following a single law that is found in its depths"; "Present reality is always in harmony with the law that is its base"; "A greater world of true reality dwells behind the present reality"; and "True reality will become present reality soon enough." These are very important words. We should contemplate them deeply and commit them to memory.

There is nothing that I can profitably add to this passage, which I have quoted in spite of its length. The next question that arises is what the Buddhist scriptures have to say about this. I quote once again:

> The Buddha said, "Good sons, I call this teaching the *Sutra of Innumerable Meanings*. The bodhisattva who wishes to practice the *Sutra of Innumerable Meanings* must realize that all dharmas are by nature empty and quiescent in nature and characteristics in the three times of past, future, and present, are neither big nor small, unborn, undying, neither dwelling nor moving, neither coming nor going, but, just like space, are nondual."
>
> The Buddha said "Good sons, that single teaching is the teaching called the *Sutra of Innumerable Meanings*. The bodhisattva who wishes to practice this teaching must first achieve an understanding of the following fact: that there is another world of great harmony, of total equality, that has been unchanging since the universe began, and that it lies behind all the things of this world. It appears as if there are all sorts of differences and changes in the world we see with our eyes. Things look large or small, as if they are coming into being or perishing, as if they are still or moving, going forward or backward. Yet at their root all are based on one true principle that penetrates all like a vacuum penetrates all things. The bodhisattva must realize that the world is one."
>
> This is the most important passage in the *Sutra of Innumerable Meanings*, as well as an extremely important passage in the understanding of the basic truth of Buddhism. Nikkyo Niwano's commentary is also very thorough. Though it is a difficult teaching, we must endeavor to study it well.

Following this, the words dharma (*ho* in Japanese),

nature (*sho*), characteristics (*so*), emptiness (*ku*), and quiescence (*jaku*) are explained, and the text moves on to the passage quoted earlier, which begins "What are the true characteristics? . . . " For the purposes of our discussion, however, we need not quote any further. The next chapter, chapter 5, is "The Essential Truths of the *Lotus Sutra*," in which the teaching of the ten suchnesses is presented. It was this book, *Bukkyo no Hongi*, from which I learned that the tenth of the ten suchness, the all embracing ultimate identity of origins and ends, has the same meaning as the *Sutra of Innumerable Meanings*.

Yet here I came to a difficult barrier. My understanding of the meaning of the *Sutra of Innumerable Meanings* by means of the words of Einstein and Yukawa was vague—I felt as if I understood and didn't really understand at the same time. I would like to quote another passage from *Bukkyo no Hongi* that supplied me with a hint as to how to resolve this remaining uncertainty.

> Observing the self objectively is essentially a matter of point of view. One must come outside of the castle of self in which one is hiding and look at oneself and others together with wide-open eyes. . . . This is called objective observation. . . . In doing this, the differences between self and other grow smaller and smaller the more one looks. For example, when you chance to pass a sumo wrestler on the street, you can't help but be a bit intimidated by the size and power of such a large fellow. Yet if you were to look down at the same scene from a helicopter one hundred meters in the air, the difference between a sumo wrestler and the average person would be very slight; and if you rose to five hundred meters, everyone would look like little ants.
>
> This is how we should observe ourselves and others, by temporarily removing ourselves from our

selves, or freeing ourselves from our selves, leaving our selves on the ground and sending a sort of incarnation up into the air in a helicopter where it can peer down and observe from a distance. This psychological function is possible for anyone, with a little practice.

When we place ourselves together with others in this way and view the scene from a distance, the difference between the self and others grows very slight. Our own feelings of inferiority disappear, as well as the feeling of intimidation by others. And the feeling "We are all in this together, it is together that we make human society" grows within us.

The feeling of great joy that is the result of gaining understanding of this truth is indescribable. It is a joy that makes one want to shout out one's gratitude. This feeling is called "resultant rejoicing" (*zuiki*) in Buddhist terminology, and when we have been invaded by the joy that comes with understanding the truth, all jealousy and envy, the petty emotions of the weakling, suddenly disappear, evaporate. If this were to happen to all people, not only would each of us be happy, but the entire world would be at peace and we would be able to make great strides. At any rate, stepping out of the shell of subjectivism and viewing the world in an objective manner is the best method for people to attain true wisdom. The highest degree of that wisdom is the wisdom of the Buddha.

With this wisdom, we can not only clearly distinguish the differences between the various phenomena in the universe, but also see the equality that lies behind them and the changes they have gone through in the past, are going through in the present, and will go through in the future, all without error, as if they were reflected in a mirror. This is the Buddha's wisdom, or the Buddha's "wisdom eye." I believe that the very best way to make ourselves happy and to assure the peace of the world and the progress of man is for everyone to learn the custom of seeing himself and others objectively.

This passage is from a section commenting on a phrase of the scripture praising the virtues of the *Sutra of Innumerable Meanings*. The passage states that the sutra will "awaken the mind of resultant rejoicing in those who are jealous." Jealousy is born from the small subjective self, so it disappears when we are able to see ourselves objectively. Not only does it disappear, but a resultant rejoicing takes its place. This is because, as we learn the practice of observing ourselves objectively, the "world of true reality that dwells behind the present reality" (in the words of Dr. Yukawa) naturally enters our hearts. The mind that can view itself objectively is a mind that can know its True Life—and that is the reason that rejoicing results. And it is in order to understand, as Einstein says, "a certain something that we cannot fully describe truly exists, and . . . that it is the supreme intelligence and of blinding beauty" that it is necessary to remove ourselves from our subjective stance at least temporarily. The "emotion" that Einstein refers to when he says "This awareness, this emotion, is the core of the true religious spirit" is what enters into our hearts after our subjectivity, our self, has been laid to rest. The emotion cannot enter when our mind is painted over with the color of subjectivity.

I feel that it is only now, as I write this, that I have understood Dogen's words, "Carrying the self along as you practice the myriad practices is ignorance; pressing forward in the myriad practices and practicing the self is enlightenment."

Though it may be anticlimactic, I would like to record

here an event that occurred long ago. It was during my convalescence, when I was completely dependent upon my parents. My father was asked by our local pharmacist to rent the room next to mine to two sisters who were commuting to pharmaceutical college. Both of these young women were very sound sleepers, and were not bothered in the least by the noise of the passing trains. Yet one night they both awoke at the same time and I heard them say that they had both dreamed of their brother back home. After expressing their hope that he was all right, they both went back to sleep. The next day a telegram from their native Gifu arrived with the message "Brother dead." Their brother's first son had just been born to him, and he had been in fine health and spirits; but while bicycling along a mountain road he had fallen over a precipice. At that time I concluded that there must be a special sympathy among the brain waves of family members.

Lately I have learned that many ardent Buddhist lay believers have had numerous, even more baffling experiences of the sort I described above. They are so varied that my theory about sympathy among family members is not sufficient, and several theories seem necessary to explain them all. I do not wish to deny the accounts of those lay believers; though modern science is considerably advanced, there remain many things which it cannot fully explain. Our five senses are clearly far from complete registers of experience—a statement that a simple comparison with the senses of other animals quickly proves.

What I wish to say is that it is a mistake for the materialist to deny the existence of any phenomenon that cannot be explained by modern science. And it is a mistake as well, because one has experienced a great many things that cannot be explained by science, to deny the validity of materialism. Materialism and religion can coexist, just as phenomena and their essences coexist as one being.

Materialism does not preclude faith. True reality lies behind present reality. Nor does faith preclude materialism. True reality presently becomes present reality.

Present reality is the form that matter takes and true reality is the being of matter and the "something" that makes matter be as it is. The greatest physicists, who have advanced far ahead of all their predecessors, are unable to approach that something which they have been in search of with anything other than the sentiments of religious awe. In this I see the limits of mankind.

And with the following passage I come to the end of this work. There are words of Christ that suggest he was a materialist, by my definition. I have already quoted them in chapter 4, but they bear repeating here:

> And when he was demanded of the Pharisees, when the Kingdom of god should come, he answered them and said, The Kingdom of God cometh not with observation:
> Neither shall they say, Lo here! or, lo there! for, behold, the Kingdom of God is within you.
>
> Luke 17:20–21

All of the words of Christ are words that flowed out from the True Life, the Great Life of the universe. All of us are living that Great Life, and its pulse throbs through our individual existences. Christ described the True Mind— the mind of the great universal life—as the mind of Jesus.

We also have words of Shakyamuni that show he might well have been a materialist. These were contained at the end of the Preface but, again, I would like to repeat them here:

> "O monks! I will teach you about the all." And he called them together and said the following. "O monks, what is the all? It is the eye and form, the ear

and sound, the nose and scent, the tongue and tatse, the body and texture, the mind and dharma. O monks, this we call the all. O monks! Should there be a person who says that he will tell you of another all beyond this all, those are only empty words, and he will be unable to reply to the criticisms of others, and he will eventually fall into difficulties. Why is that? O monks, it is because his all is not a thing of this world."

Finally, I would like to say a word about why I wrote this work, *A Materialist's Religion*. I am a follower of neither Christianity nor Buddhism; I am not a philosopher or a Buddhist scholar. I myself admit surprise at the fact that I have written a work with such a high-sounding title. It can only be because I am, in my heart, a fervent Christian, and because I have at the same time taken deep refuge in the teachings of Shakyamuni.

Knowing as I do that religious conviction and materialism are not contradictory, I am bereaved at the fact that most people, materialists whether they realize it or not, do not give religion a second thought. Believing that to be ignorant of religion is to be ignorant of one's own self, it is my hope that with this book I have brought religion to even one more person. To know the true meaning of religion is to know the True Life, to know one's own mind, and to know the true reality behind all phenomena. I refrain from becoming attached to either Christianity or Buddhism, or one of the many sects within Buddhism, simply because I am aware that at the base of every religion and every sect the same life force is to be found, the same reflections on human existence are to be discovered.